NATEF Correlated Task Sheets

for

Automotive Steering, Suspension, and Alignment

Sixth Edition

James D. Halderman

PEARSON

Boston Columbus Indianapolis New York San Francisco Upper Saddle River
Amsterdam Cape Town Dubai London Madrid Milan Munich Paris Montreal Toronto
Delhi Mexico City Sao Paulo Sydney Hong Kong Seoul Singapore Taipei Tokyo

Editor in Chief: Vernon Anthony
Acquisitions Editor: Lindsey Prudhomme Gill
Editorial Assistant: Amanda Cerreto
Director of Marketing: David Gesell
Marketing Manager: Harper Coles
Marketing Assistant: Crystal Gonzalez
Project Manager: Jessica H. Sykes
Production Manager: Holly Shufeldt
Cover Art Director: Jayne Conte

Cover Designer: Bruce Kenselaar
Editor, Digital Projects: Nichole Caldwell
Media Project Manager: Karen Bretz
Full-Service Project Management: Abinaya Rajendran, Integra Software Services, Inc.
Composition: Integra Software Services, Ltd.
Printer/Binder: Edwards Brothers Malloy
Cover Printer: Edwards Brothers Malloy
Text Font: Times New Roman

PEARSON

10 9 8 7 6 5 4 3 2 1

ISBN 10:   0-13-284524-5
ISBN 13: 978-0-13-284524-3

Contents

Fire Extinguisher

Meets NATEF Task: (None Specified)

Name _____ Date _____

Make/Model _____ Year _____ Instructor's OK [ ]

_____ 1. Describe the location of the fire extinguishers in your building or shop and note the last inspection dates.

Type of Extinguisher	Location	Inspection Date
_____	_____	_____
_____	_____	_____
_____	_____	_____
_____	_____	_____

_____ 2. Do any of the fire extinguishers need to be charged?

_____ Yes (which ones) _____

_____ No

_____ 3. Where can the fire extinguishers be recharged? List the name and telephone number of the company.

_____ _____

_____ 4. What is the cost to recharge the fire extinguishers?

a. Water = _____

b. CO_2 = _____

c. Dry chemical = _____

Vehicle Hoisting

Meets NATEF Task: (None Specified)

Name _____ Date_____

Make/Model _____ Year _____ Instructor's OK [   ]

Getting Ready to Hoist the Vehicle

_____ **1.** Drive the vehicle into position to be hoisted (lifted) being certain to center the vehicle in the stall.

_____ **2.** Pull the vehicle forward until the front tire rests on the tire pad (if equipped).

_____ **3.** Place the gear selector into the park position (if the vehicle has an automatic transmission/transaxle) or in neutral (if the vehicle has a manual transmission/transaxle) and firmly apply the parking brake.

_____ **4.** Lower the driver's side window before exiting the vehicle. (This step helps prevent keys from being accidentally being locked in the vehicle.)

_____ **5.** Position the arms and hoist pads under the frame or pinch-weld seams of the body.

Hoisting the Vehicle

_____ **6.** Slowly raise the vehicle about one foot (30 cm) off the ground and check the stability of the vehicle by attempting to move the vehicle on the lift.

_____ **7.** If the vehicle is stable and all pads are properly positioned under the vehicle, continue hoisting the vehicle to the height needed.

NOTE: Best working conditions are at chest or elbow level.

_____ **8.** Be sure the safety latches have engaged before working under the vehicle.

Lowering the Vehicle

_____ **9.** To lower the vehicle, raise the hoist slightly, then release the safety latches.

_____ **10.** Lower the vehicle using the proper operating and safety release levers.

CAUTION: Do not look away while lowering the vehicle. One side of the vehicle could become stuck or something (or someone) could get under the vehicle.

_____ **11.** After lowering the hoist arms all the way to the floor, move the arms so that they will not be hit when the vehicle is driven out of the stall.

Work Order

Meets NATEF Task: (A4-A-1) Complete work order. (P-1)

Name _____ Date _____

Make/Model _____ Year _____ Instructor's OK ☐

Fill in the customer and vehicle information, plus the customer concerns and related service history.

UAS Automotive
1415 Any Street
City, State 99999

ASE CERTIFIED — NATEF
ASE CERTIFIED PROGRAM

Customer Information
Name _____
Daytime _____ Address _____
Evening _____ City _____ State _____ Zip _____

Vehicle Information
Year _____ Model _____
Color _____ Mileage _____
VIN _____

Materials
_____
_____
_____
_____
_____
_____
_____
_____
_____
_____
_____
_____
_____
_____
_____
_____
_____

Customer Concern _____

Related Service History _____

Labor Performed _____

Root Cause of Problem _____

Totals

Materials _____
Labor _____
Misc. _____
Sub Total _____
Tax _____
TOTAL _____

Customer Authorization

X _____

Vehicle Service Information and TSBs

Meets NATEF Task: (A4-A-3) Research applicable vehicle and service information, such as suspension and steering system operation, vehicle service history, and TSBs. (P-1)

Name _____ Date _____

Make/Model _____ Year _____ Instructor's OK [   ]

_____ **1.** Vehicle and/or suspension/steering-related technical service bulletins (TSBs).

      A. Topic _____   Bulletin number _____
      Problem/correction _____

      B. Topic _____   Bulletin number _____
      Problem/correction _____

      C. Topic _____   Bulletin number _____
      Problem/correction _____

      D. Topic _____   Bulletin number _____
      Problem/correction _____

_____ **2.** Vehicle history of repair. List all suspension/steering-related repairs from customer records or repair order files.

      _____
      _____

_____ **3.** List all suspension/steering-related service precautions as published in service information.

      A. _____   E. _____
      B. _____   F. _____
      C. _____   G. _____
      D. _____   H. _____

_____ **4.** Determine the location of the following suspension/steering service information and where (books, CD, Web site) it was found.

      A. Suspension/steering torque specifications: ____ Located _____
      B. Alignment specification: _____ Located _____
      C. Tire information _____ Located _____
      D. Other (specify) _____ Located _____

Vehicle Identification Number

Meets NATEF Task: (A4-A-4) Locate and interpret vehicle and major component identification numbers. (P-1)

Name _____ **Date** _____

Make/Model _____ **Year** _____ **Instructor's OK** [ ]

VIN Number _____

- The first number or letter designates the **country of origin** = _____

1 = United States	6 = Australia	L = China	V = France
2 = Canada	8 = Argentina	R = Taiwan	W = Germany
3 = Mexico	9 = Brazil	S = England	X = Russia
4 = United States	J = Japan	T = Czechoslovakia	Y = Sweden
5 = United States	K = Korea	U = Romania	Z = Italy

- The model of the vehicle is commonly the fourth or fifth character. **Model?** _____

- The eighth character is often the engine code. (Some engines cannot be determined

  by the VIN number.) **Engine code:** _____

- The tenth character represents the year on all vehicles. See the following chart.

VIN Year Chart (The pattern repeats every 30 years.)   **Year?** _____

A = 1980/2010	J = 1988/2018	T = 1996/2026	4 = 2004/2034
B = 1981/2011	K = 1989/2019	V = 1997/2027	5 = 2005/2035
C = 1982/2012	L = 1990/2020	W = 1998/2028	6 = 2006/2036
D = 1983/2013	M = 1991/2021	X = 1999/2029	7 = 2007/2037
E = 1984/2014	N = 1992/2022	Y = 2000/2030	8 = 2008/2038
F = 1985/2015	P = 1993/2023	1 = 2001/2031	9 = 2009/2039
G = 1986/2016	R = 1994/2024	2 = 2002/2032	
H = 1987/2017	S = 1995/2025	3 = 2003/2033	

Hybrid Vehicle Electric Power Steering

Meets NATEF Task: (A4-B-21) Identify hybrid vehicle power steering system electrical circuits, service and safety precautions. (P-3)

Name _____ Date_____

Make/Model _____ Year _____ Instructor's OK ☐

_____ **1.** Check service information for the specified procedures to follow when servicing the electric power steering on a hybrid electric vehicle (HEV). Describe the recommended precautions.

_____

_____

_____ **2.** What color is the protective conduit around the wiring to the electric power steering?

____ Black (usually 12 volts)

____ Blue (usually 42 volts)

____ Yellow (usually 42 volts)

____ Orange (usually 144+ volts)

_____ **3.** Check service information for the specified tools and safety equipment specified when servicing the electric power steering system on a hybrid electric vehicle. Check all that apply.

____ CAT III meter

____ High-voltage gloves

____ Insulated tools

____ Other (describe) _____

_____

_____

_____

Hybrid High-Voltage Disconnect

Meets NATEF Task: (A6-A-21) Identify the location of hybrid vehicle safety disconnect location and safety procedures. (P-3) (P-1)

Name _____ Date _____

Make/Model _____ Year _____ Instructor's OK ☐

Hybrid electric vehicles (HEV) use a high-voltage battery pack and an electric motor(s) to help propel the vehicle. To safely work around a hybrid electric vehicle, the high-voltage (HV) battery and circuits should be shut off following these steps:

Step 1	Turn off the ignition key (if equipped) and remove the key from the ignition switch.
Step 2	Disconnect the high-voltage circuits.

CAUTION: Some vehicle manufacturers specify that rubber insulated lineman's gloves be used whenever working around the high-voltage circuits to prevent the danger of electrical shock.

Toyota Prius
The cutoff switch is located in the trunk. To gain access, remove three clips holding the upper left portion of the trunk side cover. To disconnect the high-voltage system, pull the orange handled plug while wearing insulated rubber lineman's gloves.

Ford Escape
The high-voltage shut off switch is located in the rear of the vehicle under the right side carpet.

Honda Civic
To totally disable the high-voltage system on a Honda Civic, remove the main fuse (labeled number 1) from the driver's side underhood fuse panel.

Chevrolet/GMC Pickup Truck
The high-voltage shut off switch is located under the rear passenger seat. Remove the cover marked "energy storage box" and turn the green service disconnect switch to the horizontal position to turn off the high-voltage circuits.

Material Safety Data Sheet (MSDS)

Meets NATEF Task: (None Specified)

Name _____ Date _____

Make/Model _____ Year _____ Instructor's OK [   ]

_____ **1.** Locate the MSDS sheets and describe their location

_____

_____

- **Product name** _____

        chemical name(s)

        _____

        Does the chemical contain "chlor" or "fluor" which may indicate hazardous

        materials? **Yes** _____ **No** _____

        flash point = _____ (hopefully above 140° F)

        pH _____ (7 = neutral, higher than 7 = caustic (base), lower than 7 = acid)

- **Product name** _____

        chemical name(s) _____

        Does the chemical contain "chlor" or "fluor" which may indicate hazardous

        materials? **Yes** _____ **No** _____

        flash point = _____ (hopefully above 140° F)

        pH _____ (7 = neutral, higher than 7 = caustic (base), lower than 7 = acid)

- **Product name** _____

        chemical name(s) _____

        Does the chemical contain "chlor" or "fluor" which may indicate hazardous

        materials? **Yes** _____ **No** _____

        flash point = _____ (hopefully above 140° F)

        pH _____ (7 = neutral, higher than 7 = caustic (base), lower than 7 = acid)

Tire Identification

Meets NATEF Task: (A4-A-3) Research applicable vehicle and service information, such as suspension and steering system operation, vehicle service history, and TSBs. (P-1)

Name _____ **Date** _____

Make/Model _____ **Year** _____ **Instructor's OK** ☐

_____ **1.** Check service information and determine the following tire-related information.

    A. Tire size _____

    B. Spare tire size _____

    C. Specified inflation pressure _____

    D. Spare tire inflation pressure _____

    E. Optional tire size (if any) _____

_____ **2.** Check service information and determine the following tire service-related information.

    A. Recommended tire rotation method: _____

    _____

    _____

    B. Recommended tire rotation mileage: _____

    _____

Tire Pressure Monitoring System

Meets NATEF Task: (A4-F-11) Inspect, diagnose and calibrate tire pressure monitoring system. (P-2)

Name _____ Date_____

Make/Model _____ Year _____ Instructor's OK [ ]

_____ 1. Check service information to determine the specified procedure to follow when inspecting, diagnosing, or calibrating the tire pressure monitoring system. Describe the specified procedures.

_____

_____

_____

_____ 2. With what type of TPMS is the vehicle equipped?

   ____ Indirect

   ____ Direct

   If direct-type system, what type of sensor is used?

        ____ Stem-mounted

        ____ Banded

        ____ Unknown

_____ 3. Is recalibrating the sensors needed if the tires are rotated?

        ____ Yes (If yes, what is the procedure?) _____

        _____

        ____ No

Tire Inspection and Air Loss

Meets NATEF Task: (A4-F-1 and A4-F-9) Inspect tire condition and check for loss of air pressure. (P-1)

Name _____ Date _____

Make/Model _____ Year _____ Instructor's OK ☐

_____ **1.** Inspect tire condition and inflation pressure. Record the results:

	Condition	Tread Depth	Inflation Pressure
Left front	_____	_____	_____
Right front	_____	_____	_____
Right rear	_____	_____	_____
Left rear	_____	_____	_____
Spare	_____	_____	_____

_____ **2.** Check tires for air loss. Describe the procedure used. _____

_____

_____ **3.** Based on the inspection results, what is the necessary action? _____

_____

_____

TIRE TREAD

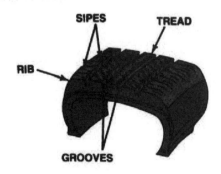

Tire Vibration and Pull Diagnosis

Meets NATEF Task: (A4-F-2 and A4-F5) Diagnose vibration and pull concerns; determine necessary action. (P-2)

Name _____ Date_____

Make/Model _____ Year _____ Instructor's OK [   ]

_____ **1.** Check service information for the specified procedures to follow when diagnosing vibration and pull concerns. Describe the recommended procedures.

_____

_____

_____ **2.** Check all that are specified:

      _____ Test drive

      _____ Use an electronic vibration analyzer (EVA)

      _____ Visual inspection

      _____ Measure radial runout _____

      _____ Measure lateral runout _____

      _____ Rotate tires

      _____ Other (describe) _____

      _____

_____ **3.** Based on the diagnostic procedures, what is the necessary action?

_____

_____

13

Tire Rotation

Meets NATEF Tasks: (A4-F-3) Rotate tires according to manufacturer's recommendations. (P-1)

Name _____ Date_____

Make/Model _____ Year _____ Instructor's OK [ ]

_____ **1.** Check the service information for the recommended tire rotation method.

          _____ Cannot rotate tires on this vehicle
          _____ Modified X method
          _____ X method
          _____ Front to rear and rear to front

LF	RF	LF	RF	LF	RF
LR	RR	LR	RR	LR	RR
RWD		**FWD**		**DIRECTIONAL**	

_____ **2.** Hoist the vehicle safely to a good working position (chest level).

_____ **3.** Remove the wheels and rotate them (if possible) according to the vehicle manufacturer's recommendation.

_____ **4.** Check and correct the tire air pressures according to the service information on the placard on the driver's door.

         Specified front tire air pressure = _____

         Specified rear tire air pressure = _____

_____ **5.** Lower the vehicle and move the hoist pads before driving the vehicle out of the service stall.

14

Tire, Wheel, Axle, and Hub Runout

Meets NATEF Tasks: (A4-F-4) Measure wheel, tire, axle flange, and hub runout; determine necessary action. (P-2)

Name _____ Date_____

Make/Model _____ Year _____ Instructor's OK ☐

_____ **1.** Check service information for the specifications for radial and lateral runout.

Specification for radial runout = _____ (usually less than 0.060 inch).

Specification for lateral runout = _____ (usually less than 0.045 inch).

_____ **2.** Using a runout gauge, rotate the tire and record the radial runout (roundness of the tires) and the lateral runout (side-to-side movement) of the tires.

Tire	Radial Runout	Lateral Runout
R.F.	_____	_____
R.R.	_____	_____
L.F.	_____	_____
L.R.	_____	_____

_____ **3.** Using a dial indicator, measure the axle and hub runout.

Hub runout   = _____   OK ____   NOT OK ____

Flange runout = _____   OK ____   NOT OK ____

CHECKING HUB RUNOUT

CHECKING MOUNTING FLANGE RUNOUT

_____ **4.** Based on the measurements, what necessary action is needed?

_____

_____

15

Install Wheel on Vehicle

Meets NATEF Task: (A4-F-8) Reinstall wheel; torque lug nuts.
(P-1)

Name _____ Date _____

Make/Model _____ Year _____ Instructor's OK [   ]

_____ **1.** Determine the vehicle manufacturer's specified lug nut torque specification.

_____ (usually between 80 and 100 lb-ft)

_____ **2.** Use a hand-operated wire brush on the wheel studs to ensure clean and dry threads and check for damage.

OK _____ **NOT OK** _____ Describe fault: _____

_____ **3.** Verify that the lug nuts are OK and free of defects.

CAUTION: Some vehicle manufacturers warn to not lubricate the wheel studs because this can cause the lug nuts to loosen while the vehicle is being driven, resulting in personal injury.

_____ **4.** Install the wheel over the studs and start all lug nuts (or bolts) by hand.

_____ **5.** Tighten the lug nuts a little at a time in a star pattern using an air impact wrench equipped with the proper torque limiting adapter or a torque wrench.

_____ Used a torque wrench

_____ Used an air impact with a torque limiting adapter

_____ **6.** Tighten the lug nuts to final torque in a star pattern.

NOTE: "Tighten one, skip one, tighten one" is the usual method if four or five lug nuts are used.

16

Tire Replacement

Meets NATEF Task: (A4-F-6 [P-1] and (A4-F-7 [P-2] Dismount and remount tire on wheel; balance.

Name _____ Date _____

Make/Model _____ Year _____ Instructor's OK [ ]

_____ **1.** Check the instructions for the proper use of the tire changer. Describe the recommended procedure.

_____

_____

_____ **2.** Check all steps that were performed.

     _____ **Removed the valve core** (TPMS equipped tire/wheel assembly; check service information for the exact procedure to follow.)

INSTALL TPMS SENSOR
FLAT SIDE DOWN

     _____ **Demount the tire from the wheel. Instructor OK** _____

     _____ **Clean bead seat.**

     _____ **Lubricate the tire bead.**

     _____ **Mount the tire and inflate** to specified inflation pressure.

_____ **3.** Balance tire/wheel assembly.

     Instructor OK _____

17

Tire Repair

Meets NATEF Task: (A4-F-10) Repair tire using internal patch. (P-1)

Name _____ Date_____

Make/Model _____ Year _____ Instructor's OK [ ]

_____ **1.** Locate the source of the leak by submerging the tire under water or by spraying the tire with soapy water. Describe the location of the leak.

_____

_____ **2.** Remove the foreign object and use a reamer to clean the hole in the tire (tread area only).

_____ **3.** Dismount the tire and buff the inside of the tire around the hole.

_____ **4.** Apply rubber cement to the buffed area.

_____ **5.** Insert the repair plug from the inside of the tire.

_____ **6.** Pull the plug through the puncture from the outside of the tire.

_____ **7.** Use a stitching tool to make sure the inside of the patch is well adhered to the inside of the tire.

_____ **8.** Remove the tire and inflate to the air pressure specified by the vehicle manufacturer.

_____ **9.** Check the repair for air leaks using soapy water.

OK ____ **NOT OK** ____

18

Suspension and Steering System Information

Meets NATEF Task: (A4-A-3) Research applicable vehicle and service information. (P-1)

Name _____ **Date** _____

Make/Model _____ **Year** _____ **Instructor's OK** ☐

Consult the service information and determine the following.

_____ **1.** List suspension-related technician service bulletins (TSBs).

        A. Topic _____ Bulletin Number _____

           Fault/Concern _____

           Corrective Action _____

        B. Topic _____ Bulletin Number _____

           Fault/Concern _____

           Corrective Action _____

_____ **2.** List all published service precautions from the service information.

        _____

        _____

_____ **3.** Research the vehicle's service history and record all suspension or steering service or repairs.

        _____

        _____

_____ **4.** Record all suspension and steering specifications.

        _____

        _____

19

Suspension Problem Diagnosis

Meets NATEF Task: (A4-A-2) Identify and interpret suspension concerns; determine necessary action. (P-1)

Name _____ Date_____

Make/Model _____ Year _____ Instructor's OK [   ]

_____ **1.** What is the stated customer concern? _____

_____ **2.** Test drive the vehicle under the same conditions and road surface types as stated by the customer when the problem occurs and check the following.

Tire-type noise?	OK _____	NOT OK _____
Clunks?	OK _____	NOT OK _____
Creaks?	OK _____	NOT OK _____
Tracks straight?	OK _____	NOT OK _____
Pull during braking only?	OK _____	NOT OK _____
Wandering (unstable)?	OK _____	NOT OK _____

Other concern (describe) _____

_____ **3.** When does the fault or concern occur?

_____ During turns or cornering to the right
_____ During turns or cornering to the left
_____ During turns or cornering both to the right or the left
_____ While driving straight ahead
_____ Only when driving on a rough road
_____ Only when turning into or out of a driveway
_____ Other (describe) _____

_____ **4.** Based on the test drive, what components or systems could be the cause of the suspension problem or concern?

_____

_____

_____ **5.** What action will be needed to correct these concerns? _____

_____

_____

20

Diagnose Suspension Concerns

Meets NATEF Task: (A4-C-1 and A4-C-2) Diagnose SLA and strut suspension concerns; determine necessary action. (P-1)

Name _____ Date_____

Make/Model _____ Year _____ Instructor's OK ☐

_____ **1.** Check service information for the specified procedures to follow when diagnosing suspension-related concerns. Check all items that are specified.

       _____ Road Test

       _____ Visual inspection

       _____ Ride height measurement

       _____ Other (describe) _____

       _____

_____ **2.** Based on the inspection, what is the necessary action? _____

_____

_____

21

Suspension Inspection/Component Replacement

Meets NATEF Task: (A4-C-3 [P-2], A4-C-5 [P-1], A4-C-6 [P-2], and A4-C-7 [P-3]
Front suspension inspection and component replacement.

Name _____ Date _____

Make/Model _____ Year _____ Instructor's OK [ ]

_____ **1.** Check service information for the exact procedures to follow when removing, inspecting, and replacing front suspension components. Describe the recommended procedures.

_____

_____

_____ **2.** Check all components that were inspected, removed or replaced.

_____ Upper control arms/bushings

_____ Lower control arms/bushings

_____ Strut rods/bushings

_____ Steering knuckle

_____ Coil springs and spring insulators

_____ **3.** Describe the reason why the parts were replaced. _____

_____

22

Strut Rod and Stabilizer Bar Bushings

Meets NATEF Task: (A4-C-4 and A4-C-9) Inspect, test, and replace thermostat and gasket/seal. (P-2)

Name _____ Date _____

Make/Model _____ Year _____ Instructor's OK ☐

_____ **1.** Check service information for the exact procedure to follow to remove, inspect, and install struts and bushings. Describe the recommended steps.

_____

_____

_____

_____

_____

_____

_____

_____ **2.** Check service information for the exact procedures to follow to remove, inspect, and install stabilizer bar bushings. Describe the recommended steps.

_____

_____

23

Torsion Bar

Meets NATEF Task: (A4-C-8) Remove, inspect, install, and adjust suspension system torsion bars; inspect mounts. (P-3)

Name _____ Date _____

Make/Model _____ Year _____ Instructor's OK [   ]

_____ **1.** Check the service information for the specified removal and reinstallation procedure.

_____

_____

_____

_____

_____ **2.** List the tools needed.

_____

_____

_____

_____

_____

_____ **3.** Check the service information and describe the proper ride height adjustment procedure.

_____

_____

_____

_____

_____

_____ **4.** Inspect the torsion bar mounts.

OK _____   **NOT OK** _____

Describe the faults and needed action.

_____

_____

TORSION BAR

TORSION BAR
ANCHOR ARM
SWIVEL
LOWER CONTROL ARM
HEIGHT ADJUSTMENT BOLT

24

MacPherson Strut Service

Meets NATEF Task: (A4-C-10) Remove, inspect, and install strut cartridge or assembly, strut coil spring, insulators (silencers), and upper strut bearing mount. (P-1)

Name _____ Date_____

Make/Model _____ Year _____ Instructor's OK

_____ **1.** Check the service information for the specified service procedure.

_____

_____

_____

_____ **2.** Safely support the vehicle on jacks and/or the lift.

_____ **3.** Remove the upper and lower attaching bolts and nuts.

_____ **4.** Carefully remove the MacPherson strut assembly from the vehicle.

_____ **5.** Compress the coil spring with the proper equipment and replace the strut assembly.

Show the instructor the disassembled unit.

Instructor's OK _____

_____ **6.** Reinstall the complete assembly.

NOTE: The vehicle should be aligned after replacing the strut assembly.

STRUT COVER

UPPER SPRING SEAT

DUST COVER

COIL SPRING

LATERAL LINK

TRAILING LINK

25

Front Shock Absorber Replacement

Meets NATEF Task: (A4-D-1) Inspect, remove, and replace
shock absorbers. (P-1)

Name _____ Date _____

Make/Model _____ Year _____ Instructor's OK [   ]

_____ 1. Verify that the front shock absorber requires replacement. Check all that apply:

_____ bent or damaged shock or mounting hardware
_____ shock absorber is leaking hydraulic fluid
_____ excessively worn - causing tire wear or riding comfort problems
_____ other (specify) _____

_____ 2. Compare the replacement shocks to the original shocks to be sure that they are correct.
OK _____ NOT OK _____
NOTE: All shock absorbers should be replaced in pairs only. Do not replace just one shock absorber.

_____ 3. Check the service information for the specified replacement procedure. _____
_____
_____

HINT: Many shocks on rear-wheel-drive vehicles can be broken off using a deep-well socket and a long extension. By rocking the extension back and forth, the top of the shock will usually break off saving the time and effort it takes to remove a nut that is often rusted in place after many years of service.

_____ 4. Safely hoist the vehicle.

_____ 5. Remove the lower shock absorber retaining bolts (nuts) as per the service information instructions..
CAUTION: Be ready to catch the shock absorber because it will likely fall after removing the last retaining bolt (nut).

_____ 6. Show the instructor the removed shock absorber. **Instructor's OK** _____

_____ 7. Extend the rod on the replacement shock and install the lower retaining bolts (nuts).

_____ 8. Lower the vehicle and install the upper retaining fastener.

_____ 9. Bounce the vehicle to check that the replacement shock does not interfere with any part of the suspension or frame.

_____ 10. Test drive the vehicle before returning it to the customer.

26

Rear Leaf Springs

Meets NATEF Task: (A4-C-11) Remove, inspect, and install leaf springs, leaf spring insulators (silencers), shackles, brackets, bushings, and mounts. (P-3)

Name _____ Date _____

Make/Model _____ Year _____ Instructor's OK [   ]

_____ **1.** Check the service information for the specified procedure for the removal and reinstallation of rear leaf springs.

_____

_____

_____

U-BOLTS

BUSHING

HANGER

EYE

PAD
RETAINER

HANGER

HANGER
PIN

PAD

BUSHING

SHACKLE

PAD

SPRING
SEAT

_____ **2.** List the tools and equipment needed. _____

_____

_____ **3.** Show the instructor the removed rear leaf spring(s). **Instructor's OK** _____

_____ **4.** List the tightening torque specifications for the affected fasteners. _____

_____

27

Shock Absorber/Strut Cartridge Replacement

Meets NATEF Task: (A4-C-10 and A4-D-1) Inspect, test, and replace thermostat and gasket/seal. (P-1)

Name _____ Date _____

Make/Model _____ Year _____ Instructor's OK [   ]

_____ **1.** Check service information for the specified procedure to follow when inspecting, removing, and replacing shock absorbers. Describe recommended steps.

_____

_____

_____ **2.** Instructor OK after removal _____

_____ **3.** Check service information for the specified procedures to follow when inspecting, removing, and replacing strut cartridges. Describe the recommended steps.

_____

_____

_____

_____

_____ **4.** Instructors OK after removal _____

29

Electronic Stability Control System ID

Meets NATEF Task: (A4-A-3) Research vehicle service information.
(P-1)

Name _____ **Date** _____

Make/Model _____ **Year** _____ **Instructor's OK** [ ]

_____ **1.** Check service information for the vehicle and check the following:

   a. Vehicle manufacturer's name of their electronic stability control system =

   _____

   b. Location of the steering wheel position sensor (describe location):

   _____

   c. Location of the lateral and/or yaw sensor (describe location):

   _____

   d. Location of the controller (computer) used to control the electronic stability
      control system (describe location):

   _____

_____ **2.** Check for any and all service precautions and technical service bulletins that are
      related to the electronic stability control system.

   _____

   _____

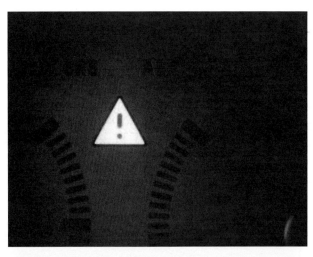

30

Airbag System and Steering Wheel Service

Meets NATEF Task: (A4-B-1 and A4-B-2) Disable and enable airbag system and center/replace the clockspring. (P-1)

Name _____ **Date** _____

Make/Model _____ **Year** _____ **Instructor's OK** ☐

_____ **1.** Check service information for the specified procedures to follow when disabling an airbag system. Check all that apply.

    _____ Disconnect the negative battery cable.

    _____ Remove the airbag fuse.

    _____ Disconnect the electrical connector(s)

    _____ Other (describe) _____

_____ **2.** Check service information for the specified procedure to follow when removing and replacing the steering wheel. Describe the recommended procedures.

_____

_____

_____ **3.** Describe the specified method to center the airbag system clockspring.

_____

_____

Airbag System and Steering Wheel Service

Meets NATEF Tasks: (B-1 and A4-B-2) (Disarming and enabling an airbag and occupant classification (OCS))

Name		Date		Time on Task	
Make/Model		Year		Instructor's OK	

1. Check service information for the specified procedure to follow when disarming an airbag system. List the tool(s) and equipment.

   Disconnect the negative battery cable.

   Remove the airbag fuse.

   Disconnect the airbag electrical connector(s).

   Wait time (describe).

2. Check service information for the specified procedure to follow when removing and installing the driver's side airbag. Describe the recommended procedure.

3. Describe the specified method to identify occupant classification system.

31

Steering Column Related Diagnosis

Meets NATEF Task: (A4-B-3 and A4-B-6) Steering column inspection and diagnosis; determine necessary action. (P-2)

Name _____ Date _____

Make/Model _____ Year _____ Instructor's OK [　　]

_____ **1.** Check service information for the specified procedures to follow when diagnosing a conventional steering gear. Describe recommended procedures.

_____

_____

_____ **2.** Check service information for the specified procedures for checking the following steering components.

_____ Universal joint - _____

_____ Flexible coupling - _____

_____ Collapsible column - _____

_____ Lock cylinder - _____

_____ Steering wheel - _____

_____ **3.** Based on the results of the inspection, what is the necessary action? _____

_____

_____

32

Steering Gear Adjustment and Replacement

Meets NATEF Task: (A4-B-7 [P-3] and A4-B8 [P-2]) Adjust non-rack and pinion worm bearing preload and sector lash; Remove and replace rack and pinion steering gear.

Name _____ **Date** _____

Make/Model _____ **Year** _____ **Instructor's OK** ☐

_____ **1.** Check service information for the specified procedure to follow to adjust a conventional steering gear assembly Describe the recommended procedure for:

Worm bearing preload - _____

_____

Sector lash (overcenter adjustment) - _____

_____

_____ **2.** Check service information for the specified procedure to follow for replacing a rack and pinion steering gear assembly. Describe the recommended procedures.

_____

_____

_____ **3.** Describe the condition of the mounting bushings and brackets. _____

_____

33

Suspension and Steering Lubrication

Meets NATEF Task: (A4-D-6) Lubricate suspension and steering system. (P-2)

Name _____ Date _____

Make/Model _____ Year _____ Instructor's OK ☐

_____ **1.** Check the service information regarding lubrication points. Describe the location.

_____

_____

_____ **2.** What is the specified grease or lubricant? _____

_____

_____ **3.** How many sealed ball and socket joints do not require lubrication?

_____

34

Steering Problem Diagnosis

Meets NATEF Task: (A4-A-2) Identify and interpret steering concerns; determine necessary action. (P-1)

Name _____ Date_____

Make/Model _____ Year _____ Instructor's OK [____]

_____ **1.** What is the stated customer concern? _____

_____ **2.** Test drive the vehicle under the same condition and road surface types as stated by the customer when the problem occurs and check the following.

Steers straight?	OK ____	NOT OK ____
Wanders?	OK ____	NOT OK ____
Noise during turns or corners?	OK ____	NOT OK ____
Hard steering when cold only?	OK ____	NOT OK ____
Hard steering when raining?	OK ____	NOT OK ____
Noise when steering?	OK ____	NOT OK ____
Looseness in steering wheel?	OK ____	NOT OK ____
Lack of steering control?	OK ____	NOT OK ____

Other concerns (describe) _____

_____

_____ **3.** When does the fault or concern occur?

____ During turns or cornering to the right
____ During turns or cornering to the left
____ During turns or cornering both to the right or the left
____ While driving straight ahead
____ Only when driving on a rough road
____ Only when turning into or out of a driveway
____ Other (describe) _____

_____ **4.** Based on the test drive, what components or systems could be the cause of the suspension problem or concern?

_____

_____

_____ **5.** What action will be needed to correct these concerns? _____

_____

_____

35

Inner Tie Rod Ends and Bellows Boots

Meets NATEF Task: (A4-B-9) Inspect and replace rack and pinion steering gear inner tie ends (sockets) and bellows boots. (P-2)

Name _____ **Date** _____

Make/Model _____ **Year** _____ **Instructor's OK** [ ]

_____ 1. Check the service information and write the specified procedure to inspect and replace the inner tie rod ends.

_____

_____

_____

_____

_____ 2. Hoist the vehicle safely and visually check the condition of the inner tie rod end bellows boots.

_____ OK
_____ Cracked in places, but not all the way through (recommend replacement)
_____ Cracked open places (requires replacement)
_____ Missing

_____ 3. Most vehicle manufacturers recommend that the entire rack and pinion steering gear assembly be removed from the vehicle when replacing the inner tie rod ends (ball socket assemblies).

_____ **Yes** (recommend that rack be removed)
_____ **No** (the tie rod end can be removed with the rack in the vehicle)

_____ 4. Describe the method used to retain the inner ball sockets to the ends of the rack.

_____ Pin
_____ Rivet
_____ Stacked
_____ Other (describe) _____

_____ 5. List all precautions found in the service information regarding this procedure.

_____

_____ 6. Describe any problems _____

36

Inspect and Replace Steering Components

Meets NATEF Task: (A4-B-17) Inspect and replace pitman arm, relay (centerlink/intermediate) rod, idler arm and mountings, and steering linkage damper. (P-2)

Name _____ Date _____

Make/Model _____ Year _____ Instructor's OK [ ]

_____ **1.** Check the service information for the specified testing and inspection procedures and specifications.

     A. Specified testing procedures: _____

     _____

     B. Specifications: _____

     _____

_____ **2.** Check the steering components listed and note their condition.

     Idler arm: _____

     _____

     Pitman arm: _____

     _____

     Centerlink: _____

     _____

     Steering linkage damper: _____

     _____

_____ **3.** State the specified replacement procedure and list any specific tools needed.

     Idler arm: Procedure _____

          Tools _____

     Pitman arm: Procedure _____

          Tools _____

     Centerlink: Procedure _____

          Tools _____

     Steering linkage damper: Procedure _____

          Tools _____

37

Tie-Rod End Inspection and Replacement

Meets NATEF Task: (A4-B-18) Inspect, replace, and adjust tie rod ends (sockets), tie rod sleeves and clamps. (P-1)

Name _____ Date_____

Make/Model _____ Year _____ Instructor's OK [ ]

_____ 1. Verify that the tie-rod end(s) requires replacement. Check all that apply.

  _____ Torn grease boot
  _____ Joint has side-to-side movement
  _____ Physically damaged
  _____ Other (specify) _____

_____ 2. Hoist the vehicle safely.

_____ 3. Compare the replacement tie-rod end with the original to be sure that the new end is correct.

_____ 4. Remove the retaining nut and use a tie-rod puller to separate the tie-rod end from the steering knuckle and/or center link.

> **HINT:** Often a hammer can be used to jar loose the tie-rod end especially if a downward force is exerted on the tie-rod while an assistant taps on the steering knuckle at the tie-rod end.

_____ 5. Measure the distance between the center of the tie-rod end and the adjusting sleeve and record this distance so the replacement tie-rod end can be installed in approximately the same location so that the wheel alignment (toe setting) will be close to being correct.

_____ 6. Unscrew the old tie-rod end and discard.

_____ 7. Install the replacement tie-rod end and adjust to the same distance as measured and recorded in #5.

_____ 8. Install the tie-rod end onto the steering knuckle and torque the retaining nut to factory specifications.

  Torque specifications for the tie-rod retaining nut = _____

_____ 9. Lower the vehicle and align the vehicle before returning it to the customer.

38

Steering Gear Diagnosis

Meets NATEF Task: (A4-B-4 and A4-B-5) Diagnose conventional and rack and pinion steering gears; determine necessary action. (P-2)

Name _____ Date_____

Make/Model _____ Year _____ Instructor's OK [ ]

_____ **1.** Check service information for the specified procedure to follow when diagnosing conventional steering gear mechanical and noise concerns. Describe the recommended procedures.

_____

_____

_____ **2.** Check service information for the specified procedures to follow when diagnosing a rack and pinion steering gear assembly. Describe the recommended procedures.

_____

_____

_____

_____ **3.** Based on the diagnosis, what is the necessary action?

_____

_____

39

Power Steering Fluid

Meets NATEF Task: (A4-B-10 [P-1] and A4-B-11 [P-2]) Determine proper fluid and flush power steering system.

Name _____ **Date** _____

Make/Model _____ **Year** _____ **Instructor's OK** [ ]

_____ **1.** Check service information for the specified fluid to use in the power steering system.

Specified fluid = _____

_____ **2.** Check service information for the specified procedure to follow when flushing, filling, and bleeding a power steering system. List the recommended steps:

Step 1 _____

Step 2 _____

Step 3 _____

Step 4 _____

40

Diagnose Power Steering Fluid Leakage

Meets NATEF Task: (A4-B-12) Diagnose power steering fluid leakage; determine necessary action. (P-2)

Name _____**Date**_____

Make/Model _____ **Year** _____ **Instructor's OK** ☐

_____ **1.** Check the service information for the specified power steering fluid.

    _____ Power steering fluid

    _____ Dexron III ATF

    _____ Type F ATF

    _____ Other (specify) _____

_____ **2.** Perform a visual inspection of the power steering system and determine the location of any leaks. Hoist the vehicle if necessary. Check each area listed below that is found to be leaking.

    _____ Pump shaft seal area

    _____ Reservoir cap

    _____ Reservoir

    _____ High-pressure line at the pump

    _____ High-pressure line between the pump and the gear

    _____ High-pressure line at the gear

    _____ Steering gear leak near the stub shaft

    _____ Steering gear leak at the inner tie rod end boots

    _____ Low-pressure hose leak (describe the location) _____

    _____ Other (describe) _____

_____ **3.** What action is necessary to correct the leak(s)? _____

_____

_____

_____

41

Service Power Steering Pump

Meets NATEF Task: (A4-B-13 [P-1], A4-B-14 [P-2], and A4-B-15 [P-2]) Remove, inspect, replace, and adjust power steering pump belt and pump; press fit pump pulley.

Name _____ Date_____

Make/Model _____ Year _____ Instructor's OK [ ]

_____ 1. Check service information for the specified procedures and specifications for removing, replacing, and adjusting the power steering pump and drive belt. Describe the recommended procedure.

_____

_____

Specified belt tension = _____

_____ 2. Remove and reinstall power steering pump assembly.   Instructor check _____

_____ 3. Check service information for the specified procedure to follow to remove and reinstall the power steering pump drive pulley. Describe the recommended procedure.

_____

_____

List the tools required. _____

Instructor check _____

42

Inspect Power Steering Hoses and Fittings

Meets NATEF Task: (A4-B-16) Inspect and replace power steering hoses and fittings.
(P-2)

Name _____ Date _____

Make/Model _____ Year _____ Instructor's OK ☐

_____ 1. Check the service information for the specified procedures, precautions, and torque specifications.

        A. Specified procedure: _____

            _____

        B. Specified precautions: _____

            _____

        C. Specified torque specifications _____

            _____

_____ 2. Check the reason why the hoses and/or fittings are being replaced.

       _____ Leaking

       _____ Worn outside cover

       _____ Possible restriction as determined by testing

       _____ Recommended when replacing pump or gear assembly

       _____ Other (specify) _____

             _____

_____ 3. Which hose(s) or fitting(s) was replaced?

       _____ High-pressure hose and fitting

       _____ Low-pressure hose and fitting

       _____ Other (specify) _____

             _____

43

Electronically Controlled Steering Systems

Meets NATEF Task: (A4-B-19 [P-3], A4-D-4 [P-3], and A4-D-5 [P-3]) Diagnose, test and diagnose components of electronically controlled steering systems using a scan tool.

Name _____ Date_____

Make/Model _____ Year _____ Instructor's OK [　　]

_____ 1. Check service information for the specified procedures to follow when using a scan tool to diagnose components of the electronically controlled steering system. Describe the recommended procedure.

_____

_____

_____ 2. What components or sensors are displayed on the scan tool that are related to the electronically controlled steering system?

_____   _____

_____   _____

_____ 3. Check service information for the specified procedures to follow when replacing components of the electronically controlled steering system. List the replaceable components and describe the specified procedures.

Replaceable components: _____

_____

Specified procedures: _____

_____

_____ 4. What is the purpose of the idle speed compensation switch used on some vehicles?

_____

44

Electric Power Steering

Meets NATEF Task: (A4-B-20) Inspect and test electric power assist steering. (P-3)

Name _____ Date _____

Make/Model _____ Year _____ Instructor's OK [____]

_____ **1.** Check service information on the specified factory inspection and testing procedure.

_____

_____

_____ **2.** Check all that apply:

    ____ Visual inspection was specified

    ____ Uses a scan tool to test

    ____ Uses a digital multimeter to test

    ____ Other (specify) _____

        _____

        _____

_____ **3.** Based on the inspection and testing of the electric assisted power steering assembly, what is the necessary action?

_____

_____

_____

45

HEV Power Steering Circuits Services

Meets NATEF Task: (A4-B-21) Identify hybrid vehicle power steering system electrical circuits, service, and safety precautions. (P-3)

Name _____ Date_____

Make/Model _____ Year _____ Instructor's OK [____]

_____ 1. Check service information for the specified service and safety precautions regarding the electric power steering system electrical circuits used on hybrid electric vehicles.

_____

_____

_____

_____ 2. The electric power steering has how many volts sent to the steering gear assembly?

____ 12 volts

____ 36 volts

____ Other (specify) _____

_____ 3. What color is the electrical conduit around the wiring to the electric power steering assembly?

____ Black

____ Yellow

____ Blue

____ Other (specify) _____

_____ 4. List all of the safety precautions specified by the vehicle manufacturer.

_____

_____

_____

46

Wheel Bearing Service

Meets NATEF Task: (A4-D-2) Remove, inspect, and service or replace front and rear wheel bearings. (P-1)

Name _____ Date_____

Make/Model _____ Year _____ Instructor's OK [ ]

_____ 1. Remove the wheel cover and the hub dust cap (grease cap).

_____ 2. Remove and discard the cotter key.

_____ 3. Remove the spindle nut, washer and outer bearing.

_____ 4. Remove inner and outer bearing and grease seal.

_____ 5. Thoroughly clean the bearing in solvent and denatured alcohol or brake cleaner and blow it dry with compressed air.

_____ 6. Closely inspect the bearing for wear or damage.

_____ 7. Show the instructor the cleaned bearing.　　**Instructor's OK** _____

_____ 8. Repack the bearing with the correct type of wheel bearing grease.

_____ 9. Install a new grease seal using a seal installing tool.

_____ 10. Correctly adjust the bearing preload. State the specified procedure. _____

_____

_____ 11. Install the hub dust cap (grease cap) and wheel cover.

_____ 12. If a sealed wheel bearing is being replaced, what is the specified procedure and torque values?

_____

_____

47

CV Joint Noise and Vibration Diagnosis

Meets NATEF Task: (A3-D-1) Diagnose constant-velocity (CV) joint noise and vibration concerns; determine necessary action. (P-1)

Name _____ Date_____

Make/Model _____ Year _____ Instructor's OK [ ]

_____ 1. Check service information for the specified procedure that should be followed when diagnosing CV joint noise and/or vibration concerns.

_____

_____

_____ 2. Check all that were specified:

    ___ Drive backward while turning   ___ Drive in a circle to the left and right

    ___ Drive forward while turning   ___ Drive at highway speed

    ___ Drive forward straight ahead   ___ Drive in reverse straight ahead

    ___ Other (specify) _____

_____ 3. Most vehicle manufacturers specify that the engine and transmission/transaxle mounts be checked for damage or wear. What are the conditions of the mounts?

_____

_____ 4. Based on the inspection and testing, what is the necessary action? _____

_____

48

CV Joint Service

Meets NATEF Task: (A3-D-4) Inspect, service, and replace shafts, yokes, boots, and CV joints. (P-1)

Name _____ Date_____

Make/Model _____ Year _____ Instructor's OK [   ]

_____ **1.** Check service information and determine the specified procedures, tools, and torque specification needed to service CV joints.

Specified procedure: _____

_____

Tools/equipment: _____

_____

Torque specification: _____

_____ **2.** Following the specified procedure, remove the drive axle shaft assembly.

Instructor's check _____

_____ **3.** Following the specified installation procedure, check all that were replaced.

___ Drive axle shaft assembly   ___ CV joint and boot

___ CV joint boot only   ___ Other (specify) _____

_____ **4.** Reinstall the drive axle shaft assembly.

Instructor's OK _____

49

Steering and Suspension Concerns

Meets NATEF Task: (A4-D-1) Diagnose vehicle wander, drift, pull, hard steering, bump steer, memory steer, torque steer; determine necessary action. (P-1)

Name _____ Date_____

Make/Model _____ Year _____ Instructor's OK [   ]

_____ **1.** Check the service information to determine the alignment specifications.

Camber = _____ Caster = _____ Toe = _____

_____ **2.** Hoist the vehicle on the alignment rack and install the wheel sensors.

_____ **3.** Compensate the wheel sensors.

_____ **4.** Lower the vehicle and jounce (bounce) to center the suspension.

_____ **5.** Read the rear camber and toe.

	LR	RR
Camber	_____	_____
Toe	_____	_____

Total rear toe = _____

_____ **6.** Read the front camber and toe.

	LF	RF
Camber	_____	_____
Toe	_____	_____

Total front toe = _____

_____ **7.** Perform a caster sweep to determine the front caster and SAI.

	LF	RF
Caster	_____	_____
SAI	_____	_____

Based on the alignment angles, what action is needed? _____

_____

50

Alignment Specification

Meets NATEF Task: (A4-A-3) Research applicable vehicle and service information, such as suspension and steering system operation, vehicle history, and TSBs. (P-1)

Name _____ Date_____

Make/Model _____ Year _____ Instructor's OK [　　]

_____ **1.** Find the following alignment angle specifications for your vehicle:

Camber (left) preferred = _____ minimum _____ maximum _____

Camber (right) preferred = _____ minimum _____ maximum _____

Caster (left) preferred = _____ minimum _____ maximum _____

Caster (right) preferred = _____ minimum _____ maximum _____

Front toe preferred = _____ minimum _____ maximum _____

Rear camber preferred = _____ minimum _____ maximum _____

Total rear toe preferred = _____ minimum _____ maximum _____

_____ **2.** Determine the diagnostic angle specifications for your vehicle:

Toe-out on turn (TOOT) inside wheel = _____ degrees

outside wheel = _____ degrees

Maximum allowable variation = _____ degrees

Steering axis inclination (SAI) left = _____

right = _____

Maximum allowable difference = _____

51

Pre-Alignment Inspection

Meets NATEF Task: (A4-E-2) Perform prealignment inspection and measure vehicle ride height; perform necessary action. (P-1)

Name _____ Date _____

Make/Model _____ Year _____ Instructor's OK [   ]

_____ **1.** Check tires. Both front tires and both rear tires should be checked for the following:

    A. Correct tire pressure

    B. Same size and brand

    C. Same tread depth

    OK _____ NOT OK _____

_____ **2.** Perform a dry-park test to check for any looseness in the steering and suspension components such as:

    A. Tie rods

    B. Idler arms

    C. Ball-joints

    D. Control arm bushings

    E. Loose or defective wheel bearings

    OK _____ NOT OK _____

_____ **3.** Check for proper ride height.

    A. Front and rear

    B. Left and right

    OK _____ NOT OK _____

52

Alignment Angle Readings

Meets NATEF Task: (A4-E-3) Prepare vehicle for wheel alignment on the alignment machine; perform four-wheel alignment by checking and adjusting wheel caster. (P-1)

Name _____ Date_____

Make/Model _____ Year _____ Instructor's OK [   ]

_____ **1.** Hoist the vehicle on the alignment rack and install the wheel sensors.

_____ **2.** Compensate the wheel sensors as per the alignment equipment manufacturer's recommended procedure.

_____ **3.** Lower the vehicle and jounce (bounce) to center the suspension.

_____ **4.** Read the rear camber and toe.

	LR	RR
Camber	_____	_____
Toe	_____	_____

Total rear toe = _____

_____ **5.** Read the front camber and toe.

	LF	RF
Camber	_____	_____
Toe	_____	_____

Total front toe = _____

_____ **6.** Perform a caster sweep to determine the front caster and SAI.

	LF	RF
Caster	_____	_____
SAI	_____	_____

Describe what (if anything) is wrong with the present alignment.

_____

53

Four-Wheel Alignment

Meets NATEF Tasks: (A4-E-3) Prepare vehicle for wheel alignment on the alignment machine; perform four-wheel alignment by checking and adjusting wheel caster. (P-1)

Name _____ Date _____

Make/Model _____ Year _____ Instructor's OK [   ]

Specifications:	Left	Right
Camber	_____	_____
Caster	_____	_____
Toe (Total)		_____
KPI/SAI		_____
Rear Camber	_____	_____
Rear Toe	_____	_____
Rear Toe (Total)		_____

Methods of Adjustment:	Front	Rear
Camber	_____	_____
Caster	_____	
Toe	_____	_____

Reading Before Alignment: (Record here and attach the print out.)

	Left	Right
Camber	_____	_____
Caster	_____	_____
Toe (Total)		_____
KPI/SAI		_____
Rear Camber	_____	_____
Rear Toe		_____
Thrust		_____
Set Back		_____

Reading After Alignment: (Record here and attach the print out.)

	Left	Right
Camber	_____	_____
Caster	_____	_____
Toe (Total)		_____
KPI/SAI		_____
Rear Camber	_____	_____
Rear Toe		_____
Thrust		_____
Set Back		_____

54

TOOT and SAI

Meets NATEF Task: (A4-E-4 [P-2]and A4-E-5 [P-2]) Check toe-out-on-turns (turning radius) and SAI (steering axis inclination) and included angle; determine necessary action.

Name _____ Date _____

Make/Model _____ Year _____ Instructor's OK [ ]

_____ **1.** Check the alignment equipment instructions and measure the toe-out-on-turns.

        LEFT TOOT   **RIGHT TOOT**

        _____   _____

_____ **2.** Check service information for the specified toe-out-on-turns (TOOT).

        Specifications = _____

_____ **3.** Based on the TOOT readings, what is the necessary action?

        _____

        _____

_____ **4.** Check steering axis inclination (SAI) and compare to factory specifications.

        SAI LEFT   **SAI RIGHT**

        _____   _____

        Specification for SAI = _____

_____ **5.** Based on the SAI reading, what is the necessary action?

        _____

        _____

        _____

        _____

55

Diagnostic Alignment Angles

Meets NATEF Task: (A4-E-6 [P-1], A4-E-7 [P-2]), and A4-E8 [P3]) Check angles that can detect collision damage; determine necessary action.

Name _____ Date _____

Make/Model _____ Year _____ Instructor's OK [   ]

_____ **1.** Measure the rear thrust angle and compare it to factory specifications.

Measured rear thrust angle = _____

Specified thrust angle = _____

_____ **2.** Based on the results of the rear thrust angle measurement, what is the necessary action.?

_____

_____

_____ **3.** Measure the front wheel setback and compare it to factory specifications.

Measured front wheel setback = _____

Specified front wheel setback = _____

_____ **4.** Based on the results of the front wheel setback measurement, what is the necessary action.?

_____

_____

_____ **5.** Check service information for the specified location and dimensions to check for the proper alignment of the front and/or rear cradle (subframe).

_____

_____

_____ **6.** Based on the results of the measurements, compared to factory specifications, what is the necessary action?

_____

56

Noise and Vibration Diagnosis

Meets NATEF Tasks: (A4-F-2) Diagnose wheel/tire vibration, shimmy, and noise; determine necessary action. (P-2)

Name _____ Date_____

Make/Model _____ Year _____ Instructor's OK [   ]

_____ **1.** Check service information for the specified (if any) methods and procedures to follow when diagnosing noise and/or vibration concerns.

_____

_____

_____ **2.** Test drive the vehicle and verify the concerns. Check all that apply:

___ Noise   ___ Vibration   ___ Both

_____ **3.** If there is a vibration, what frequency and at what speed is the vibration?

Frequency _____   Vehicle speed _____

Frequency _____   Vehicle speed _____

Frequency _____   Vehicle speed _____

Frequency _____   Vehicle speed _____

_____ **4.** If a noise, check for witness marks and describe this location: _____

_____

_____ **5.** Based on the test results and visual inspection, what is the necessary action?

_____

APPENDIX

2012 NATEF Correlation Chart (A4)

MLR-Maintenance & Light Repair
AST-Auto Service Technology (Includes MLR)
MAST-Master Auto Service Technology (Includes MLR and AST)

	SUSPENSION AND STEERING (A4)						
	Task	**Priority**	**MLR**	**AST**	**MAST**	**Text Page #**	**Task Page #**
General: Suspension and Steering Systems							
1.	Research applicable vehicle and service information, vehicle service history, service precautions, and technical service bulletins.	P-1	✓	✓	✓	4	4
2.	Identify and interpret suspension and steering system concerns; determine necessary action.	P-1			✓	160–161	19; 34
Steering Systems Diagnosis and Repair							
1.	Disable and enable supplemental restraint system (SRS).	P-1	✓	✓	✓	229–230	30
2.	Remove and replace steering wheel; center/time supplemental restraint system (SRS) coil (clock spring).	P-1		✓	✓	402	30
3.	Diagnose steering column noises, looseness, and binding concerns (including tilt mechanisms); determine necessary action.	P-2		✓	✓	230–235	31
4.	Diagnose power steering gear (non-rack and pinion) binding, uneven turning effort, looseness, hard steering, and noise concerns; determine necessary action.	P-2		✓	✓	292–296	38
5.	Diagnose power steering gear (rack and pinion) binding, uneven turning effort, looseness, hard steering, and noise concerns; determine necessary action.	P-2		✓	✓	292–293	32

	Task	Priority	MLR	AST	MAST	Text Page #	Task Page #
6.	Inspect steering shaft universal-joint(s), flexible coupling(s), collapsible column, lock cylinder mechanism, and steering wheel; perform necessary action.	P-2		✓	✓	230	31
7.	Remove and replace rack and pinion steering gear; inspect mounting bushings and brackets.	P-2		✓	✓	300–302	36
8.	Inspect rack and pinion steering gear inner tie rod ends (sockets) and bellows boots; replace as needed.	P-2	✓ Inspect only (P-1)	✓	✓	266	35
9.	Determine proper power steering fluid type; inspect fluid level and condition.	P-1	✓	✓	✓	294	39
10.	Flush, fill, and bleed power steering system.	P-2	✓	✓	✓	294–295	39
11.	Inspect for power steering fluid leakage; determine necessary action.	P-1	✓	✓	✓	293	40
12.	Remove, inspect, replace, and adjust power steering pump drive belt.	P-1	✓	✓	✓	292–293	41
13.	Remove and reinstall power steering pump.	P-2		✓	✓	297	41
14.	Remove and reinstall press fit power steering pump pulley; check pulley and belt alignment.	P-2	✓ Check/adjust PS belt (P-1)	✓	✓	297	41
15.	Inspect and replace power steering hoses and fittings.	P-2	✓	✓	✓	297	42
16.	Replace power steering pump filter(s).	P-1	✓ (P-2)	✓	✓	297	42
17.	Inspect and replace pitman arm, relay (centerlink/intermediate) rod, idler arm and mountings, and steering linkage damper.	P-2	✓ (P-1)	✓	✓	260–262	36
18.	Inspect, replace, and adjust tie rod ends (sockets), tie rod sleeves, and clamps.	P-1	✓	✓	✓	263–265	37

	Task	Priority	MLR	AST	MAST	Text Page #	Task Page #
19.	Test and diagnose components of electronically-controlled steering systems using a scan tool; determine necessary action.	P-3	✓ Inspect electric power steering only	✓	✓	287–291	43
20.	Identify hybrid vehicle power steering system electrical circuits and safety precautions.	P-2	✓	✓	✓	287–290	44; 45
Suspension Systems Diagnosis and Repair							
1.	Diagnose short and long arm suspension system noises, body sway, and uneven ride height concerns; determine necessary action.	P-1		✓	✓	155; 159–161	19; 20
2.	Diagnose strut suspension system noises, body sway, and uneven ride height concerns; determine necessary action.	P-1		✓	✓	159	19; 20
3.	Inspect, remove and install upper and lower control arms, bushings, shafts, and rebound bumpers.	P-3	✓ Inspect and replace rebound and jounce bumper only (P-1)	✓	✓	174–175	21
4.	Inspect, remove and install strut rods and bushings.	P-3	✓	✓	✓	174	24
5.	Inspect, remove and install upper and/or lower ball joints (with or without wear indicators).	P-2	✓ Inspect only (P-1)	✓	✓	162–167	21
6.	Inspect, remove and install steering knuckle assemblies.	P-3		✓	✓	177	21
7.	Inspect, remove and install short and long arm suspension system coil springs and spring insulators.	P-3	✓ Inspect only (P-1)	✓	✓	174–176	21
8.	Inspect, remove and install torsion bars and mounts.	P-3	✓ Inspect only (P-1)	✓	✓	177	23
9.	Inspect, remove and install front stabilizer bar (sway bar) bushings, brackets, and links.	P-3	✓ Inspect only (P-1)	✓	✓	173	22

	Task	Priority	MLR	AST	MAST	Text Page #	Task Page #
10.	Inspect, remove and install strut cartridge or assembly, strut coil spring, insulators (silencers), and upper strut bearing mount.	P-3	✓ Inspect only (P-1)	✓	✓	170–172	24
11.	Inspect, remove and install track bar, strut rods/radius arms, and related mounts and bushings.	P-3	✓ Inspect only (P-1)	✓	✓	192	21
12.	Inspect rear suspension system leaf spring(s), bushings, center pins/bolts, and mounts.	P-1		✓	✓	194	26
13.	Inspect electric power-assisted steering.	P-3	✓	✓	✓	287–290	43
Related Suspension and Steering Service							
1.	Inspect, remove, and replace shock absorbers; inspect mounts and bushings.	P-1	✓	✓	✓	170; 193	25
2.	Remove, inspect, and service or replace front and rear wheel bearings.	P-1		✓	✓	311–316	46
3.	Describe the function of the power steering pressure switch.	P-3	✓	✓	✓	284–285	38
Wheel Alignment Diagnosis, Adjustment, and Repair							
1.	Diagnose vehicle wander, drift, pull, hard steering, bump steer, memory steer, torque steer, and steering return concerns; determine necessary action.	P-1		✓	✓	357; 377–381	49
2.	Perform pre-alignment inspection and measure vehicle ride height; perform necessary action.	P-1	✓	✓	✓	378	51
3.	Prepare vehicle for wheel alignment on alignment machine; perform four-wheel alignment by checking and adjusting front and rear wheel caster, camber; and toe as required; center steering wheel.	P-1		✓	✓	384	52; 53
4.	Check toe-out-on-turns (turning radius); determine necessary action.	P-2		✓	✓	385	54

	Task	Priority	MLR	AST	MAST	Text Page #	Task Page #
5.	Check SAI (steering axis inclination) and included angle; determine necessary action.	P-2		✓	✓	385	54
6.	Check rear wheel thrust angle; determine necessary action.	P-1		✓	✓	388	53
7.	Check for front wheel setback; determine necessary action.	P-2		✓	✓	372	52
8.	Check front and/or rear cradle (subframe) alignment; determine necessary action.	P-3		✓	✓	388	55
Wheels and Tires Diagnosis and Repair							
1.	Inspect tire condition; identify tire wear patterns; check for correct tire size and application (load and speed ratings) and adjust air pressure; determine necessary action.	P-1		✓	✓	64–65; 99	9; 11
2.	Diagnose wheel/tire vibration, shimmy, and noise; determine necessary action.	P-2		✓	✓	106–111	12
3.	Rotate tires according to manufacturer's recommendations.	P-1	✓	✓	✓	104–105	13
4.	Measure wheel, tire, axle flange, and hub runout; determine necessary action.	P-2		✓	✓	106–109	14
5.	Diagnose tire pull problems; determine necessary action.	P-2		✓	✓	379	12
6.	Dismount, inspect, and remount tire on wheel; balance wheel and tire assembly (static and dynamic).	P-1	✓	✓	✓	101–102; 116–118	16
7.	Dismount, inspect, and remount tire on wheel equipped with tire pressure monitoring system sensor.	P-2	✓	✓	✓	101	10
8.	Inspect tire and wheel assembly for air loss; perform necessary action.	P-1	✓	✓	✓	99	11
9.	Repair tire using internal patch.	P-1	✓	✓	✓	113–115; 119–120	17

	Task	Priority	MLR	AST	MAST	Text Page #	Task Page #
10.	Identify and test tire pressure monitoring system (indirect and direct) for operation; calibrate system; verify operation of instrument panel lamps.	P-2	✓	✓	✓	90–94	10
11.	Demonstrate knowledge of steps required to remove and replace sensors in a tire pressure monitoring system.	P-1	✓ (P-2)	✓	✓	89–95	10